THE EDUCATOR'S

MATCHBOOK

MANDY FROEHLICH

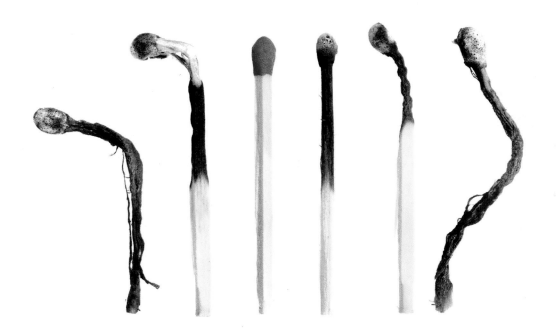

A WEEKLY GUIDE TO REIGNITING YOUR LOVE OF TEACHING, BUILDING RESILIENCE, AND FIGHTING BURNOUT AND DISENGAGEMENT.

The Educator's Matchbook
By Mandy Froehlich
Published by EduMatch®
PO Box 150324, Alexandria, VA 22315

www.edumatch.org

sarah@edumatch.org

ISBN-13: 978-1-953852-00-7

Why This Book

After writing *Reignite the Flames: Finding our passion and purpose for learning among the embers*, I spoke with friends of mine who felt disengaged that told me, "Mandy. We read your blog. We try to follow what you're saying. We just don't feel like we are getting any better." The issue is that there is no guidebook for becoming re-engaged or staying engaged in education and it can be a long, hard fought battle to get back to loving your profession again. But, nobody tells you that. The question, "How you come back from burnout?" or "How do you avoid burnout?" makes it sound like an easy fix. There is no easy fix. It's a very personal journey that takes time.

This book is not going to "fix" you either. It will, however, give you researched and proven methods to move forward in your journey. There are opportunities for reflection and practicing skills that will help rewire your brain. Like with any activity or opportunity for learning, you will get out of it what you put in. Especially in the case of educator engagement, happiness is a choice that you need to make and you need to make it every day. That also means that you need to do the good work it takes to re-engage and these activities will reap long-term benefits. They create changes that, if followed-up on, will build a foundation of gratitude, resilience, mindfulness, core beliefs, and purpose that will better equip you for challenging events in the future.

Make the choice to begin the journey and develop new habits to make you a happier person. Start letting go of the negativity that builds up and weighs you down. It's time to reignite the flame.

Reignite the Flames: Preface

I can still remember the smell of my first classroom when I walked into it. The odor could be described as somewhere amidst the orange solvent they used for cleaning, the wax on the hallway floors that was wafting in, and the musty old building. It was my favorite combination. I didn't love every day of my job, and I didn't love every task I was assigned, but I did love teaching. I loved teaching so much that I did everything everyone asked of me. When I was able to take on more and do it well, I was asked to do more and I did it because I knew it was good for the students even though I was tired and crabby with my own family when I got home. When people said, you're going to get burnt out, I said, "That's impossible. You can't get burnt out doing something you love." But, you can. Too much of anything is still too much.

The person who said, "The hardest part is getting started," never woke up one day and decided that the profession that they had considered to be their life's calling was the same thing that was bleeding them emotionally dry. That moment for me was infinitely more difficult than getting started. When I began teaching I had energy and endorphins and youth. When I disengaged and burnt out, I had growing kids of my own, not enough caffeine, and achy bones. I swear you age at two-times the rate as a teacher. And I was so unhappy.

If you would ask me what success is, I would say it is being happy...whatever happiness means to that person. Continuing to grow and be better, yet still being content with how far you've come. I'd describe success as knowing you've made a positive difference in someone else's life. You understand what you bring to the table while still remaining humble. Success is looking back on your life wishing you could do it all again the exact same way. And yet, being disengaged from your work or life isn't a way to do that. Engagement is a choice. Re-engagement is work. But, I don't see any other way to be happy and feel successful within my scope of what happiness is. I don't see how losing your purpose can leave you with a life you'd do all over again.

The journey of discovering my own disengagement and researching the causes has given me a much more empathetic lens towards my fellow educators who are having the same feelings and experiences possibly without even knowing it. It has made me more patient with those who have disengaged and made a target of their negativity. It has made me more aware of those who are starting to lose the light in their eyes and who have lost the magic—those who are tired and want out. It has made me reflect upon myself, my words, and my actions to understand how my own thinking impacts myself and those around me. It has made me want to support others because I feel like, at the end of the day, we all deserve and have the right to feel one of the most basic human emotions: happiness.

How to Use this Book

Being engaged in our jobs, especially as an educator, is one of the most powerful, grounding feelings we can have. Unfortunately, because education is so emotionally taxing and intense, engagement can be one of the first things to go if we aren't careful. I know this because I was that educator several years ago. It took me time, patience, and determination to get myself out of the disengagement hole I had fallen into. However, I learned some valuable lessons and this guide is meant to help you learn some of the strategies and reflect on the questions that I had to figure out by myself along the way.

The first part of this book will give you information on engagement and disengagement and provide you with some definitions of words that will be commonly used throughout the book. I suggest reading it first because that way you'll have the information you need to proceed. The second part is a weekly guide for you to fill out as you go. There are 14 weeks worth of goal setting and reflection meant to be done consecutively, but I purposely left the week dates blank so you can use it as you see fit.

The Weekly Page
On the first page of each week you'll start with planning out your self-care routine. You may want to have your calendar handy so you can schedule sacred self-care time. Choose (at least) one self-care activity for physical, intellectual, spiritual, and emotional self-care. Then, choose a practical self-care activity and a new self-care activity that you've never tried before. These can overlap with the four types if you'd like, but don't need to. You'll find examples for each of these categories in Part I.

WEEKLY SELF-CARE

PHYSICAL (BODY)	INTELLECTUAL (MIND)	PRACTICAL SELF-CARE:
SPIRITUAL (CENTERED)	EMOTIONAL (BALANCED)	SOMETHING NEW TO TRY:

How to Use this Book

Next, you'll plan two goals and one boundary you want to set for the week to accomplish and stick to. Have more to do then two goals? I get it. There are probably a million goals we could write down weekly. Create two goals you don't need to do but really want to get done. Something that would make you feel accomplished to check it off. Boundaries are important to maintain for our emotional health. Understanding and setting boundaries holds ourselves and others accountable for not to be taken advantage of. Setting boundaries and making them clear also lets other people know what they need to respect. You can't expect others to respect your boundaries if you don't know what they are. Set one a week but feel free to continue to work on that boundary from the previous week if you feel like it's something you struggle with.

TWO GOALS:

ONE BOUNDARY:

Next, you are going to look forward into your schedule and see if there is anything you anticipate as a struggle for you for the week. Maybe there's not enough time to make your daughter's birthday cupcakes. Maybe it's a meeting with your administrator that you're dreading. Maybe you're looking at everything you wrote down for self-care and have no idea how to fit it in. The struggle section is for you to have a plan for whatever you foresee being an issue. Creating a plan for difficult situations can relieve stress when you are able to anticipate multiple options you have to solve the problem.

To fill this part out list the struggle you're focusing on. Then, write all potential solutions no matter how ridiculous they seem. Finally, write down the solution you'd actually like to try. If that solution doesn't work, you can return to the page and choose a different potential solution. You'll have a list to choose from!

AN ANTICIPATED STRUGGLE THIS WEEK

STRUGGLE	ALL POTENTIAL SOLUTIONS	SOLUTION TO TRY

How to Use this Book

An improvement from last week asks you to reflect on something that went well - whether it was a plan in your guide, a situation you handled well, or maybe certain negative emotions you were feeling that are now improving. Don't see an improvement from the following week? Write down something that brought you joy or made you happy. We are looking for positivity here.

AN IMPROVEMENT FROM LAST WEEK

Finally, you will take an emotion dipstick. How do you feel overall? Feel free to write reasons why in the margins. This will be important as you look back through the book. Were there events that tended to make you feel a certain way? A time of the year? What triggers you to be happy or sad? You'll track your emotions twice a week. At the end of the book you'll be asked to go back through and see if you find any overarching themes with your weekly emotions. The goal of the emotion tracker is to help you identify emotional triggers so you can be better prepared to react to them.

EMOTION TRACKING:
HOW ARE YOU FEELING RIGHT NOW?

Free Your Mind
The Free Your Mind page is meant to be a brain dump. You are welcome to write anything in this space that comes to you: to do lists, feelings you have about certain things, draw pictures...the idea is to get everything out of your head and onto paper so you have more headspace to work with. Get it all out and move through the week knowing that your starting with a clean slate.

Weekly Journal
Journaling is an important way to organize your thoughts into a way that makes sense enough to get it down on paper. Each weekly journal has optional prompts to get you to reflect on your own thoughts and emotions, but feel free to write about whatever you want. Maybe it's professional. Maybe it's personal. Maybe it switches between the two. Writing is a powerful way to work through anything you feel like you need to process, especially adversities or traumas we may have experienced.

How to Use this Book

Mindfulness, Gratitude, or Resilience Practice

Each week there is an introduction to a mindfulness, gratitude, or resilience practice for you to try for your toolbox. Many times we are asked to practice these things but nobody knows exactly what to do. The practices are simple and for the most part do not take a lot of time.

Gratitude Journal

The Gratitude Journal is there to help you remember to practice gratitude every day. Ideally, you'd write down three things you're grateful for, but if that's difficult start with one. The most important part is to sit for a second and step into the feeling of gratitude. Notice what it feels like. Let it fill you up from your toes to your nose.

Mindfulness Journal

Whereas the Gratitude Journal is for writing down what you're gratuitous for, the Mindfulness Journal is for tracking what you did as a mindfulness practice. Potentially, it's the Mindfulness activity for the week or maybe you stick to one mindfulness practice for an extended period, like meditation, because it's working for you. Plan ahead for what you're doing for the week if that works or track it day-by-day if that works better for you. It doesn't need to take a great deal of time. Some days, even meditating for five minutes is something to be proud of. Use the emotion tracker in the Mindfulness journal to keep track of how the practice has made you feel.

Educator Activity

The Educator Activity is meant to be a planning or reflection tool for who you have been, who you are, and who you want to be in the profession. This is important especially if you're feeling disconnected or untethered to being an educator. It is still important to consider these reflections if you are feeling connected in order to build resilience for challenging times. Understanding who you are is one guard against burnout and demoralization. It is also one of the most important pieces for coming back from them. The Educator Activity is the only activity that may take you time to complete as they can be questions that warrant processing time. Give them their due reflection. It will help you in the long run.

How to Use this Book

Weekly Wrap-Up

The Weekly Wrap-Up is about reflecting on how the week went both personally and professionally. It gives space for reflection on most items that you planned in the beginning of the week. Be sure to find time to celebrate the pieces that went well. Is there anything you feel you need more practice on that you want to bring into the following week? While time is tight, be sure to spend some times truly and deeply reflecting on these pieces. It's where the change happens.

You'll wrap up the week with another emotion check. Feel free to write anything down, good or bad, that might help you remember why you were feeling that way at that time. The more you self-reflect, the better and more proficient you will become at self-reflection.

YOUR OVERALL IMPRESSION OF THE WEEK

REFLECTION ON TWO GOALS

REFLECTION ON BOUNDARIES

Part I: Engagement

Developing a Common Language

We throw around a lot of concepts and words in education that we usually don't take the time to define them so we are all on the same page. To give you the greatest chance at utilizing this book the best you can, Part I includes definitions and information on terms and concepts that I will be utilizing throughout. I will add in additional commentary as well to aid you in understanding the depth of importance that may of the concepts play in your everyday life even outside of education.

Educator Engagement: Intentionally seeking purpose and understanding our impact, living within that purpose, and creating opportunities for both ourselves and others to be happier, healthier, and more positively, emotionally engaged people in order to best serve those around us (Reignite the Flames, 2020).

Educator Disengagement: The unintentional detaching of oneself from the emotional connection to the why behind education and teaching due to negative factors and/or circumstances that feel out of one's control. This results in an otherwise uncharacteristically negative view of their efficacy, jobs, and potentially their personal selves (Reignite the Flames, 2020).

A few years ago when I first began discussing educator engagement people would often get defensive. They would either assume that I was talking about how much effort they put into their professional learning opportunities (being engaged in the learning) or that I was blaming them for the negativity they were feeling. The truth is that with educator disengagement there is usually not only one cause and blame really doesn't make anyone feel better. It can be a multitude of reasons why one disengages. Unfortunately, however, just because it's not your fault doesn't mean it's not your responsibility to heal. If you're waiting for an administrator to re-engage you (EVEN if you ARE an administrator and are looking to your leadership) it's not going to happen. It is a choice, made by you, to put in the good work. There are five reasons I've determined that can lead to educator disengagement. They include: personal adversity, professional adversity, burnout, secondary traumatic stress, demoralization, and teacher trauma. A more thorough description of each of these can be found in Reignite the Flames. As always, I encourage everyone to understand how this happens. Many times engagement is couched under "burnout", but there is much, much more to it than that.

Part I: Engagement

The Continuum of Educator Engagement: The Continuum of Educator Engagement was created to show that there are various degrees of engagement and disengagement. Similarly to how the educator engagement/disengagement definitions were developed by integrating the psychological term of emotional engagement with teaching, the continuum references this concept as well. Emotional engagement can be positive or negative, the latter resulting in "emotional engagement with a negative emotional attachment" - meaning that you can still be emotionally engaged with something if you are angry. You can still be passionately fighting for a cause in which you believe, therefore, still emotionally attached. To be disengaged or emotionally detached means you're most likely feeling apathy. In this case, the opposite of happy isn't sad. It's not caring.

This continuum highlights for me the emotional needs of educators but also how closely educator engagement is linked to the climate and culture of a building. Think about your colleagues. Where would they fall? What is the climate and culture of your building like?

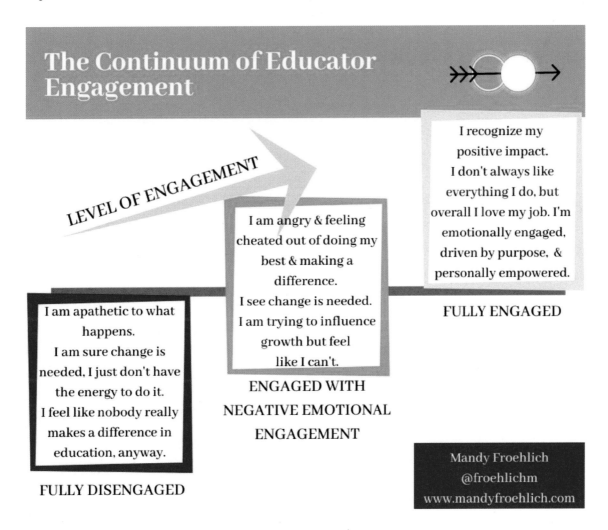

Part I: Mental Health & Self-Care

Mental Health: Defined by mentalhealth.gov as "(including) our emotional, psychological, and social well-being." Although it's been a taboo topic for awhile, we ALL have mental health. Our desire, obviously, is for it to be healthy and thriving. Like physical health, it needs intentional care and nourishment. For a long time this kind of care has been seen as unnecessary and only for people who were either not busy or lazy. Contrary to that belief, if we don't take care of our mental health there can be negative consequences.

"If you do not make time for your wellness,
you'll be forced to make time for your illness."
-Joyce Sunada

Mental Health Issues: Mental illness, also called mental health disorders, refers to a wide range of mental health conditions — disorders that affect your mood, thinking and behavior. Examples of mental illness include depression, anxiety disorders, schizophrenia, eating disorders and addictive behaviors (Mayoclinic.org). The term "mental illness" is slowly becoming replaced by the more accepted and sensitive "mental health issues." My first book *The Fire Within* begins the dive into destigmatizing educator mental health issues, and *Reignite the Flames* begins to go deeper into my research on engagement and disengagement which can be linked back to mental health issues.

Self-Care: Taking care of ourselves is necessary so we can take care of others. This isn't a platitude. It isn't a quote on a popular meme. It is a fact. I've found that people who usually poo poo self-care do it because they 1) don't understand what it really does for our bodies and minds or 2) are embarrassed to admit that they don't really know what to do beyond a good yoga session. Self-care is one way to build resilience. It provides your mind and body a solid foundation that is more prepared for struggle. That's why it's important to practice self-care EVEN if you're not feeling particularly stressed. It's like building a muscle. You need to keep working it so it's strong when you need it.

Part I: Types of Self-Care

Four Types of Self-Care: I've narrowed down four types of self-care: physical, intellectual, emotional, and spiritual. I've included some "practical self-care activities" as well.

Physical Self-Care - **Taking care of your body**

- Exercise/sports: Yoga, running, swimming, hiking, softball, soccer, dancing
- Walking the dog
- Horseback riding
- Gardening

Practical Physical Self-Care

- Attending to dental needs
- Staying hydrated and eating healthy
- Getting regular physicals
- Taking control of health issues like diabetes

Photo by Ketut Subiyanto from Pexels

Photo by RF._studio from Pexels

Intellectual Self-Care - **Taking care of your mind**

- Play board games
- Read a newspaper/news online
- Complete a crossword
- Read or listen to a book
- Learn to knit, crochet, sew a quilt, fish, surf, use Google Calendar or any other new skill you're dying to try.

Practical Intellectual Self-Care

- Learn a new budgeting technique or debt reduction system
- Teach your child something you're passionate about (teaching stimulates your brain)

Part I: Types of Self-Care

Emotional Self-Care - Finding your balance

- See a counselor (appropriate even when you're not struggling)
- Keep a journal
- Spend time with friends who make you laugh
- Learn to accept a compliment
- Practice positive self-talk

Sometimes, emotional self-care means letting toxic pieces of your life go:

- Avoid toxic people
- Set boundaries
- Practice forgiveness and let go of guilt

Practical Emotional Self-Care

- Tidy up or develop better organizational skills to reduce stress

Photo by cottonbro from Pexels

Spiritual Self-Care - Finding your center

- Practice deep reflection through writing or meditation
- Commune with nature
- Keep a gratitude journal
- Choose a day you won't complain
- Make peace with your past

Practical Spiritual Self-Care

- Volunteer for a cause you love
- Develop skills for living mindfully
- Change your mindset around challenges and failures; view them as an opportunity for growth (research Solutions Mindset or Solution-Based Thinking)

Part I: Resilience & Mindfulness

Resilience: Resilience is defined by the American Psychological Association (apa.org) as "the process of adapting well in the face of adversity, trauma, tragedy, threats, or significant sources of stress—such as family and relationship problems, serious health problems, or workplace and financial stressors." In regards to resilience, people often use the term "bouncing back" to who you were before, but I've always disagreed with this assessment having been through adversity and trauma myself. I believe that resilience is how well you adapt to those scenarios but I don't believe that you will ever be that same person again. You will be different and that is okay. You will be smarter and more aware. Less likely to make mistakes in the future. You may experience post-traumatic growth which are positive changes and growth that happen after a trauma. You will probably not, however, be the same person. If that is your goal you may feel frustrated that it's not happening, so it's important to understand that it's more about accepting and loving the new person you've become.

There are strategies for building resilience in this book: self-care, mindfulness, gratitude, goal-setting, and the practices of reflective writing and journaling.

Mindfulness: Particularly in regards to trauma, self-awareness is one of the ways we recognize emotions and the way our bodies feel and create understanding of those sensations. Mindfulness has two major elements: awareness and attention; both which are practiced nonjudgmentally. Jon Kabat-Zinn describes mindfulness as, "One way to think of this process of transformation is to think of mindfulness as a lens, taking scattered and reactive energies of your mind and focusing them into a coherent source of energy for living, for problem solving, for healing."

Practicing mindfulness calms down your sympathetic nervous system, so you are less likely to be thrown into a survival strategy. It has been shown to have a positive effect on depression, anxiety, and chronic pain. Studies have also found that it activates the brain regions involved in emotional regulation and can lead to changes in body awareness and fear, making it less likely to react to triggers (The Body Keeps Score, Van Der Kolk, 2015).

Part I: Gratitude & Boundaries

Gratitude: Practicing gratitude is a part of living mindfully. When you practice gratitude you are in the moment feeling positive and thankful for something in your life that brings you happiness or joy. Practicing gratitude or even thinking positively actually causes changes our brain. Our brains will wire themselves according to whatever you do most. There is no moral judgment in how the brain wires itself. Think of a tennis player practicing their serve. The brain doesn't say, "That's a terrible serve, I'm going to choose not to remember that." Instead, the more you practice the more hardwired that serve becomes no matter how good (or bad) it is. Positivity or gratitude and negativity are the same way. Your brain will continue to rewire itself for whatever you do most. Therefore, if you are practicing gratitude you will continue to feel thankful and blessed. That's why it's important to intentionally practice gratitude every day.

Boundaries: PositivePsychology.com defines boundaries as: "Healthy boundaries can serve to establish one's identity. Specifically, healthy boundaries can help people define their individuality and can help people indicate what they will and will not hold themselves responsible for." Learning to set healthy boundaries is an important part of self-care and building resilience. The first steps in developing boundaries are:

1. Identify desired boundary.
2. Communicate what you need.
3. Don't over-explain.
4. Say why it's important.

If you've ever told families that you won't answer calls/emails after 5pm, that would be an example of setting a boundary. Boundaries are important for a healthy work/life balance and healthy relationships.

Advantages of Healthy Boundaries

GOOD MENTAL HEALTH

INFLUENCE OTHERS' BEHAVIOR

GOOD EMOTIONAL HEALTH

AVOIDANCE OF BURNOUT

DEVELOPED AUTONOMY

DEVELOPED IDENTITY

PositivePsychology.com

Part 2
The Weekly Engagement Guide

"Be confused, it's where you begin to learn new things.
Be broken, it's where you begin to heal.
Be frustrated, it's where you start to make
more authentic decisions.
Be sad, because if we are brave enough
we can hear our heart's wisdom through it.

Be whatever you are right now.
No more hiding.
You are worthy, always."

-S.C. Lourie

WEEK OF:

WEEKLY SELF-CARE

PHYSICAL
(BODY)

INTELLECTUAL
(MIND)

PRACTICAL SELF-CARE:

SPIRITUAL
(CENTERED)

EMOTIONAL
(BALANCED)

SOMETHING NEW TO TRY:

TWO GOALS:

ONE BOUNDARY:

AN ANTICIPATED STRUGGLE THIS WEEK

STRUGGLE	ALL POTENTIAL SOLUTIONS	SOLUTION TO TRY

AN IMPROVEMENT FROM LAST WEEK

EMOTION TRACKING:
HOW ARE YOU FEELING RIGHT NOW?

FREE YOUR MIND

This page is for a brain dump. Note anything you have on your mind, make doodles, sketches, or Sketchnotes. Use it to organize your thoughts and empty your brain to make space.

WEEKLY JOURNAL

Optional Journal Prompt: Describe your favorite moment from last week in "small moment" style. Include as many descriptors as possible paying special attention to how the moment made you feel.

_____

_____

_____

_____

_____

_____

_____

_____

_____

_____

_____

_____

_____

_____

_____

_____

_____

_____

_____

_____

_____

_____

NEW GRATITUDE PRACTICE: GRATITUDE JOURNALS

Gratitude journals are simply an organized way to write down what you're gratuitous for. They don't actually need to be anything fancy. Some gratitude journals have prompts to help you reflect deeper, but from the standpoint of practicing gratitude, any blank notebook has the potential to be turned into a gratitude journal.

An important piece of gratitude journaling is allowing the feeling of gratitude fill you up as you focus on what you are thankful for. Sitting in the feeling and recognizing that gratitude can make you feel uplifted will help you later conjure that same feeling when you need the uplift.

The benefits of gratitude journaling are*:
1. Gratitude journaling, like many gratitude practices, can lower your stress levels.
2. It can help you feel calmer, especially at night.
3. Journaling can give you a new perspective on what is important to you and what you truly appreciate in your life.
4. By noting what you are grateful for, you can gain clarity on what you want to have more of in your life, and what you can do without.
5. Gratitude journaling can help you find out and focus on what really matters to you.
6. Keeping a gratitude journal helps you learn more about yourself and become more self-aware.
7. On days when you feel blue, you can read through your gratitude journal to readjust your attitude and remember all the good things in your life.

What you feel grateful for doesn't need to be only the big ticket items. You can be grateful for your car, your job, your family, and your home but you can also show gratitude for the walk you took that day, for the small plant you bought at the store, or for reaching a little further on that one difficult yoga pose. The beauty of this journaling is that it's totally what feels right to you.

*From positivepsychology.com

GRATITUDE JOURNAL

Each day write something that you are grateful for. As you write it, sink into the feeling you get when you think of it. Close your eyes. Allow the feeling to fill you up from your head to your toes.

MONDAY

TUESDAY

WEDNESDAY

THURSDAY

FRIDAY

SATURDAY

SUNDAY

NEW MINDFULNESS PRACTICE:
MINDFUL COLORING

If mindful means "being aware, in the moment, with intention and without judgment" then mindful coloring is practicing being in the moment without judgment while applying color to a picture. Typically, that picture is an intricate pattern. Oftentimes, a Mandala is shown as a pattern that feels soothing and is intricate enough to keep your attention for the 15-20 minute activity.

Benefits of mindful coloring*:
- Your brain experiences relief by entering a meditative state.
- Stress and anxiety levels have the potential to be lowered.
- Negative thoughts are expelled as you take in positivity.
- Focusing on the present helps you achieve mindfulness.
- Unplugging from technology promotes creation over consumption.

Choose a pattern you'd like to color. Using crayons or colored pencils focus on the coloring. If your mind wanders to other topics, simply acknowledge them and pull your attention back to the paper.

*From colorit.com

MINDFULNESS PLAN & REFLECTION

Create a mindfulness plan for the week. Are there mindfulness activities that you know work for you? Is there something you would like to try? As you complete each day, focus on how it made you feel. Try not to think about HOW it went. Remember, a key ingredient of mindfulness is "without judgment."

MONDAY

TUESDAY

WEDNESDAY

THURSDAY

FRIDAY

SATURDAY

SUNDAY

EDUCATOR ACTIVITY: BUILDING A JOY KIT

A joy kit, sometimes also known as a healing kit or happiness kit, is a package of items you curate to remind you of the feeling of joy when you're feeling down or stressed. You can keep it at home or at school to pull out in times of need.

What you need:

- A box -It doesn't need to be fancy. It could be an old cigar box or a shoe box. Big enough to hold your items but small enough to fit into a drawer.

Your potential joy items:

- Photos of people or memories that make you happy
- Greeting cards people have sent you
- Candles, essential oils, or other aromatherapy items
- Your favorite candies, chocolates, gum, or treats
- A small mindful coloring sheet with crayons
- A gift card to your favorite restaurant to treat yourself on those days
- A note from a student that made you feel good
- Trinkets with special meaning
- Spiritual belief items like a cross, healing crystals, or scripture

How to use the kit
Joy kits can be used anytime you need a minute to focus on happiness and joy. They can be used during times of stress, but they can also be used as a preventative measure to stress. Bonnie St. John, author of Micro-Resilience, deems joy kits one way to build micro-resilience.

When the moment feels right take out the joy kit. Go through each item one-by-one and focus on how they make you feel. Let the feeling of joy fill you up. Close your eyes if you'd like and think about the item. Allow yourself to smile or feel any emotion that comes up. When you are ready put the joy kit back for another day. If your joy kit includes treats, don't forget to periodically refill it. It won't be very joyful if you go in for an emergency piece of chocolate and remember that you already ate it!

WEEKLY WRAP-UP

This page is about reflection. Reflect in whichever way makes the most sense to you. Maybe you write sentences, make notes, or draw. The purpose is to think about how your week went, any triggers you notice, or activities that went well.

YOUR OVERALL IMPRESSION OF THE WEEK

REFLECTION ON TWO GOALS

REFLECTION ON BOUNDARIES

REFLECTION ON YOUR ANTICIPATED STRUGGLE/SOLUTION:

SOMETHING FROM THE WEEK THAT MADE YOU HAPPY:

SOMETHING FROM THE WEEK YOU WANT TO DISCONTINUE:

EMOTION TRACKING: HOW ARE YOU FEELING RIGHT NOW?

AN ARROW CAN
ONLY BE SHOT BY
PULLING IT BACKWARD.
SO, WHEN LIFE IS DRAGGING
YOU BACK WITH DIFFICULTIES,
IT MEANS THAT IT'S
GOING TO LAUNCH YOU
INTO SOMETHING GREAT.
SO JUST FOCUS,
AND KEEP AIMING.

-PAULO COELHO

WEEK OF:

WEEKLY SELF-CARE

PHYSICAL (BODY)	INTELLECTUAL (MIND)	PRACTICAL SELF-CARE:
SPIRITUAL (CENTERED)	EMOTIONAL (BALANCED)	SOMETHING NEW TO TRY:

TWO GOALS:

ONE BOUNDARY:

AN ANTICIPATED STRUGGLE THIS WEEK

STRUGGLE	ALL POTENTIAL SOLUTIONS	SOLUTION TO TRY

AN IMPROVEMENT FROM LAST WEEK

EMOTION TRACKING:
HOW ARE YOU FEELING RIGHT NOW?

FREE YOUR MIND

This page is for a brain dump. Note anything you have on your mind, make doodles, sketches, or Sketchnotes. Use it to organize your thoughts and empty your brain to make space.

WEEKLY JOURNAL

Optional Journal Prompt: Describe an event that felt like it could end negatively but ultimately ended with surprisingly positive outcomes. What did it feel like when you realized it wasn't as bad as it seemed?

_____

_____

_____

_____

_____

_____

_____

_____

_____

_____

_____

_____

_____

_____

_____

_____

_____

_____

_____

_____

_____

_____

_____

GRATITUDE JOURNAL

Each day write something that you are grateful for. As you write it, sink into the feeling you get when you think of it. Close your eyes. Allow the feeling to fill you up from your head to your toes.

MONDAY

TUESDAY

WEDNESDAY

THURSDAY

FRIDAY

SATURDAY

SUNDAY

NEW MINDFULNESS PRACTICE: LOVING KINDNESS MEDITATION

To practice self-love and kindness for others, try this meditation.

Lay quietly.
Notice your breath.
Become aware of your breath and follow it through the complete cycle of inhale and exhale-all the way through your nostrils down into your lungs and back out again. If your mind wanders, gently bring it back. Place your left hand over your heart and set the intention of being kind to yourself.

Repeat three times.
May I be happy.
May I be healthy.
May I be at peace.

Bring to mind someone you love **and repeat the following three times:**
May you be happy.
May you be healthy.
May you be at peace.

Bring to mind someone who you've had conflict with **and repeat the following three times:**
May you be happy.
May you be healthy.
May you be at peace.

Bring to mind the image of a stranger **and repeat the following three times.**
May you be happy.
May you be healthy.
May you be at peace.

Look at the world as a whole. **Repeat the following three times.**
May we be happy
May we be healthy
May we be at peace

When you're ready slowly open your eyes. When it feels right, sit up and notice how you feel from the experience.

MINDFULNESS PLAN & REFLECTION

Create a mindfulness plan for the week. Are there mindfulness activities that you know work for you? Is there something you would like to try? As you complete each day, focus on how it made you feel. Try not to think about HOW it went. Remember, a key ingredient to mindfulness is "without judgment."

MONDAY

TUESDAY

WEDNESDAY

THURSDAY

FRIDAY

SATURDAY

SUNDAY

EDUCATOR ACTIVITY: REMEMBERING YOUR FIRST DAY

There is something about the first day of school that is so special, especially when that first day is the one where you walked into your very own classroom for the first time. Take some time to recall that day. Go through the five senses. What did you smell? Hear? How did you feel? What were you thinking? Did you meet anyone? What was the first thing you did when you walked in? Why was it special?

_____

_____

_____

_____

_____

_____

_____

_____

_____

_____

_____

_____

_____

_____

_____

_____

_____

_____

_____

_____

_____

WEEKLY WRAP-UP

This page is about reflection. Reflect in whichever way makes the most sense to you. Maybe you write sentences, make notes, or draw. The purpose is to think about how your week went, any triggers you notice, or activities that went well.

YOUR OVERALL IMPRESSION OF THE WEEK

REFLECTION ON TWO GOALS

REFLECTION ON BOUNDARIES

REFLECTION ON YOUR ANTICIPATED STRUGGLE/SOLUTION:

SOMETHING FROM THE WEEK THAT MADE YOU HAPPY:

SOMETHING FROM THE WEEK YOU WANT TO DISCONTINUE:

EMOTION TRACKING: HOW ARE YOU FEELING RIGHT NOW?

THE LOTUS FLOWER RISES
FROM THE MUD AND WATER TO
BLOOM BRIGHTLY.

IT IS REGARDED AS A SYMBOL OF
PURITY, ENLIGHTENMENT,
SELF-REGENERATION
AND REBIRTH.

IT'S A PERFECT ANALOGY FOR
HUMAN ADVERSITY - EVEN THE
MUDDIEST OF ROOTS AND WATERS
CAN PRODUCE THE MOST
BEAUTIFUL FLOWER.

Photo by NEOSiAM 2020 from Pexels

WEEK OF:

WEEKLY SELF-CARE

PHYSICAL (BODY)	**INTELLECTUAL** (MIND)	**PRACTICAL** **SELF-CARE:**
SPIRITUAL (CENTERED)	**EMOTIONAL** (BALANCED)	**SOMETHING NEW** **TO TRY:**

TWO GOALS:

ONE BOUNDARY:

AN ANTICIPATED STRUGGLE THIS WEEK

STRUGGLE	ALL POTENTIAL SOLUTIONS	SOLUTION TO TRY

AN IMPROVEMENT FROM LAST WEEK

EMOTION TRACKING:
HOW ARE YOU FEELING RIGHT NOW?

FREE YOUR MIND

This page is for a brain dump. Note anything you have on your mind, make doodles, sketches, or Sketchnotes. Use it to organize your thoughts and empty your brain to make space.

WEEKLY JOURNAL

Optional Journal Prompt: Describe a day where you get to do whatever you want to do. The sky is the limit and money isn't an issue. You don't even have to write sub plans! What would you do?

_____

_____

_____

_____

_____

_____

_____

_____

_____

_____

_____

_____

_____

_____

_____

_____

_____

_____

_____

_____

_____

_____

_____

NEW GRATITUDE PRACTICE: GRATITUDE STONES

The premise of a gratitude stone is fairly simple: they are trigger object - a physical reminder to practice gratitude.

To use gratitude stones, first find a stone you like. It can be a stone you just find on the side of the road or some shoppes carry pretty stones that can be purchased. Try to find a relatively smooth one so if you keep it in a pocket it doesn't hurt.

Then, carry the stone with you. Keep it in your pocket, purse, desk, car...any place where you are going to encounter it often. Throughout the day whenever you see or feel the stone stop and think about something you're grateful for. It could be the sunrise you're looking at or the yummy lunch you just had. It could be a co-worker or the time you were given to practice meditation that morning.

Continue this practice every time you encounter the stone. Remember to allow the feeling of gratitude to fill you up from your toes to your nose.

Some people find that carrying a stone is cumbersome and there's really no place to put it where you'll encounter it on a regular basis. As a substitute, change the lock screen on your phone to a gratitude reminder (maybe a picture of a rock!) and complete the exercise every time your lock screen shows.

GRATITUDE JOURNAL

Each day write something that you are grateful for. As you write it, sink into the feeling you get when you think of it. Close your eyes. Allow the feeling to fill you up from your head to your toes.

MONDAY

TUESDAY

WEDNESDAY

THURSDAY

FRIDAY

SATURDAY

SUNDAY

MINDFULNESS PLAN & REFLECTION

Create a mindfulness plan for the week. Are there mindfulness activities that you know work for you? Is there something you would like to try? As you complete each day, focus on how it made you feel. Try not to think about HOW it went. Remember, a key ingredient to mindfulness is "without judgment."

MONDAY

TUESDAY

WEDNESDAY

THURSDAY

FRIDAY

SATURDAY

SUNDAY

EDUCATOR ACTIVITY:
YOUR EDUCATOR IDENTITY

One of the ways to root yourself to being an educator is to understand your identity as one. We often know who we are as individuals...wife, husband, mother, father, sister, tennis player, crafter, football coach, cook. Educator is usually one of the descriptors that we use to define our personal identity. But, who are you as an educator? What are your professional strengths? Passions? What brings you joy in a day? If you could spend all day teaching or doing one thing, what would it be? What do you want to learn more about? What are you so darn good at and you wish more people would notice? Try to find your identity here. Don't be afraid to write what you can and come back to it when you've had time to process.

_____

_____

_____

_____

_____

_____

_____

_____

_____

_____

_____

_____

_____

WEEKLY WRAP-UP

This page is about reflection. Reflect in whichever way makes the most sense to you. Maybe you write sentences, make notes, or draw. The purpose is to think about how your week went, any triggers you notice, or activities that went well.

YOUR OVERALL IMPRESSION OF THE WEEK

REFLECTION ON TWO GOALS

REFLECTION ON BOUNDARIES

REFLECTION ON YOUR ANTICIPATED STRUGGLE/SOLUTION:

SOMETHING FROM THE WEEK THAT MADE YOU HAPPY:

SOMETHING FROM THE WEEK YOU WANT TO DISCONTINUE:

EMOTION TRACKING: HOW ARE YOU FEELING RIGHT NOW?

ROCK BALANCING IS AN ART FORM THAT CAN HAVE BOTH A SPIRITUAL CONNECTION AND MEDITATIVE QUALITIES.

THE IDEA IS TO USE BALANCE AND COUNTERBALANCE TO CREATE STRUCTURES THAT SEEM IMPROBABLE.

MANY PEOPLE USE THIS AS A FORM OF MEDITATION AS IT'S EASY TO GET LOST IN THE TASK AND THE MOMENT.

Photo by Shiva Smyth from Pexels

WEEK OF:

WEEKLY SELF-CARE

PHYSICAL (BODY)	INTELLECTUAL (MIND)	PRACTICAL SELF-CARE:
SPIRITUAL (CENTERED)	EMOTIONAL (BALANCED)	SOMETHING NEW TO TRY:

TWO GOALS:

ONE BOUNDARY:

AN ANTICIPATED STRUGGLE THIS WEEK

STRUGGLE	ALL POTENTIAL SOLUTIONS	SOLUTION TO TRY

AN IMPROVEMENT FROM LAST WEEK

EMOTION TRACKING:
HOW ARE YOU FEELING RIGHT NOW?

FREE YOUR MIND

This page is for a brain dump. Note anything you have on your mind, make doodles, sketches, or Sketchnotes. Use it to organize your thoughts and empty your brain to make space.

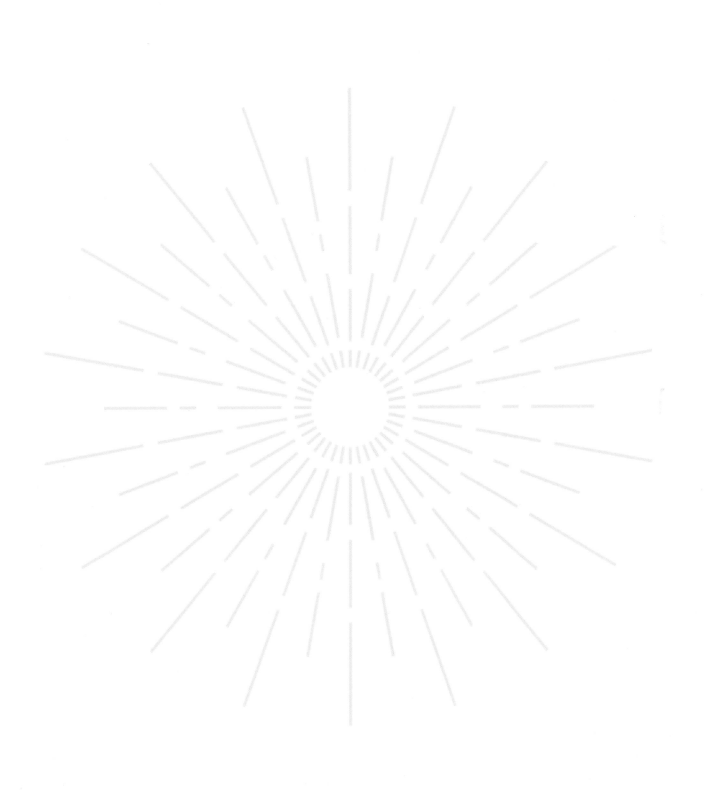

WEEKLY JOURNAL

Optional Journal Prompt: If you could pick a theme song for your life, what would it be? Why? Has it changed over time?

GRATITUDE JOURNAL

Each day write something that you are grateful for.
As you write it, sink into the feeling you get when
you think of it. Close your eyes. Allow the feeling to
fill you up from your head to your toes.

MONDAY

TUESDAY

WEDNESDAY

THURSDAY

FRIDAY

SATURDAY

SUNDAY

NEW MINDFULNESS PRACTICE: SENTENCE STEMS

The sentence stem activity asks you to add-on to the ends of phrases to make a sentence. Let your thoughts flow and don't think too much about what you want to put down. Just answer them with the first thought that comes to you.

Example: If I'm more accepting of my faults...my anxiety about being perfect would lessen.

Each group of sentence stems should be completed every day for five days. Don't spend more than three minutes a day on this activity.

If I am more accepting of my faults...

1

2

3

4

5

If I am more accepting of my fears...

1

2

3

4

5

By bringing 10% more attention to my self-care needs...

1

2

3

4

5

Reflection
Look at the answers that you provided over the course of the five days and answer this question:
If even some of the written responses are accurate, it would serve me well to...

MINDFULNESS PLAN & REFLECTION

Create a mindfulness plan for the week. Are there mindfulness activities that you know work for you? Is there something you would like to try? As you complete each day, focus on how it made you feel. Try not to think about HOW it went. Remember, a key ingredient to mindfulness is "without judgment."

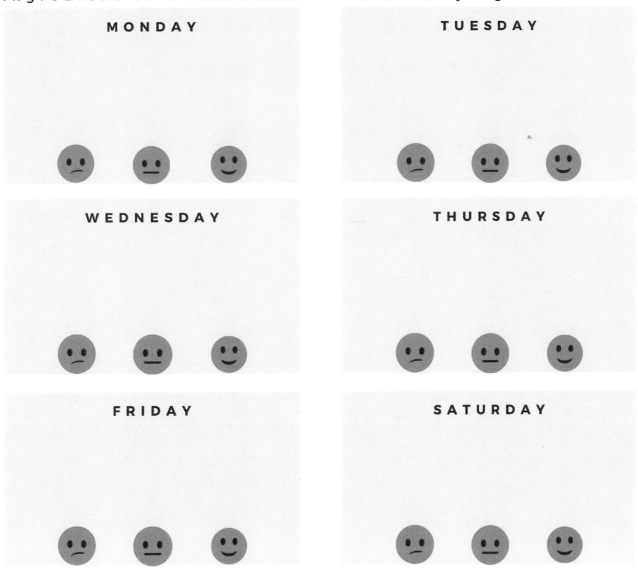

MONDAY

TUESDAY

WEDNESDAY

THURSDAY

FRIDAY

SATURDAY

SUNDAY

EDUCATOR ACTIVITY:
THE CONTINUUM OF ENGAGEMENT

Take a moment to review The Continuum of Educator Engagement in Part I. Read the descriptions for the levels of engagement and then reflect on where you think you are. Has it changed since the beginning of your career? Does it change from month-to-month? What are the contributing factors for you placing yourself where you did? How does it make you feel knowing where you are?

_____

_____

_____

_____

_____

_____

_____

_____

_____

_____

_____

_____

_____

_____

_____

_____

_____

_____

_____

WEEKLY WRAP-UP

This page is about reflection. Reflect in whichever way makes the most sense to you. Maybe you write sentences, make notes, or draw. The purpose is to think about how your week went, any triggers you notice, or activities that went well.

YOUR OVERALL IMPRESSION OF THE WEEK

REFLECTION ON TWO GOALS

REFLECTION ON BOUNDARIES

REFLECTION ON YOUR ANTICIPATED STRUGGLE/SOLUTION:

SOMETHING FROM THE WEEK THAT MADE YOU HAPPY:

SOMETHING FROM THE WEEK YOU WANT TO DISCONTINUE:

EMOTION TRACKING:
HOW ARE YOU FEELING RIGHT NOW?

A COMMON PLACE WE GET
VITAMIN D IS FROM THE SUN.
MANY PEOPLE EXPERIENCE THE
"WINTER BLUES" WHEN OUR
ACCESS TO THE SUN'S RAYS ARE
LACKING. HOWEVER, A VITAMIN D
DEFICIENCY CAN ACTUALLY BE
LINKED TO DEPRESSION, FATIGUE,
BONE ACHES, AND MUSCLE ACHES.
GETTING ENOUGH VITAMIN D IN
OUR FOOD OR TAKING A
SUPPLEMENT MIGHT BE ONE WAY
TO HELP SEASONAL
MOOD CHANGES.

WEEK OF:

WEEKLY SELF-CARE

PHYSICAL
(BODY)

INTELLECTUAL
(MIND)

**PRACTICAL
SELF-CARE:**

SPIRITUAL
(CENTERED)

EMOTIONAL
(BALANCED)

**SOMETHING NEW
TO TRY:**

TWO GOALS:

ONE BOUNDARY:

AN ANTICIPATED STRUGGLE THIS WEEK

STRUGGLE

ALL POTENTIAL SOLUTIONS

SOLUTION TO TRY

AN IMPROVEMENT FROM LAST WEEK

EMOTION TRACKING:
HOW ARE YOU FEELING RIGHT NOW?

FREE YOUR MIND

This page is for a brain dump. Note anything you have on your mind, make doodles, sketches, or Sketchnotes. Use it to organize your thoughts and empty your brain to make space.

WEEKLY JOURNAL

Optional Journal Prompt: Talk about your favorite strength. It doesn't need to be your greatest strength, maybe it's one that gives you personal satisfaction or was hard won. Why is it your favorite? What does the strength bring to your life?

_____

_____

_____

_____

_____

_____

_____

_____

_____

_____

_____

_____

_____

_____

_____

_____

_____

_____

_____

_____

_____

_____

_____

_____

NEW GRATITUDE PRACTICE: DIGGING IN DEEPER

Keeping in mind that gratitude is about the feeling, the prompts below try to guide you in thinking wider or deeper about areas you may not have thought of before.

Lessons you've been grateful for:

1.

2.

3.

Things in your life you may take for granted:

1.

2.

3.

Wishes you had that didn't come true (and the better thing that happened instead):

1.

2.

3.

A time in your life that you may reminisce about and are just glad it happened:

1.

2.

3.

GRATITUDE JOURNAL

Each day write something that you are grateful for.
As you write it, sink into the feeling you get when
you think of it. Close your eyes. Allow the feeling to
fill you up from your head to your toes.

MONDAY

TUESDAY

WEDNESDAY

THURSDAY

FRIDAY

SATURDAY

SUNDAY

MINDFULNESS PLAN & REFLECTION

Create a mindfulness plan for the week. Are there mindfulness activities that you know work for you? Is there something you would like to try? As you complete each day, focus on how it made you feel. Try not to think about HOW it went. Remember, a key ingredient to mindfulness is "without judgment."

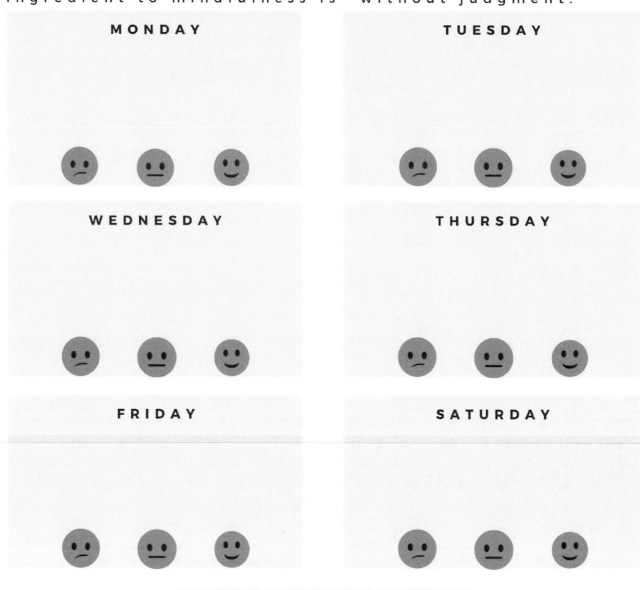

MONDAY

TUESDAY

WEDNESDAY

THURSDAY

FRIDAY

SATURDAY

SUNDAY

EDUCATOR ACTIVITY: WHAT YOU CAN CONTROL

If you often find you're frustrated with situations going on around you or if you feel like you're trapped with no choices, breaking situations down and understanding what you can control can help. Of course, this involves both recognizing what you can control AND letting go of what you can't.

You can repeat this activity as many times as you need with as many situations as you want. This is your first practice page. In every situation you have at least one choice, even if that choice is just controlling how you react. However, dig deep and think innovatively. Do you have any other choices?

SITUATION:

WHAT DO YOU HAVE CONTROL OVER?

WHAT IS OUT OF YOUR CONTROL?

WHAT OPTIONS DO YOU HAVE?

HOW WOULD IT FEEL TO LET THE PARTS YOU CAN'T CONTROL GO? HOW CAN YOU DO THAT?

WEEKLY WRAP-UP

This page is about reflection. Reflect in whichever way makes the most sense to you. Maybe you write sentences, make notes, or draw. The purpose is to think about how your week went, any triggers you notice, or activities that went well.

YOUR OVERALL IMPRESSION OF THE WEEK

REFLECTION ON TWO GOALS

REFLECTION ON BOUNDARIES

REFLECTION ON YOUR ANTICIPATED STRUGGLE/SOLUTION:

SOMETHING FROM THE WEEK THAT MADE YOU HAPPY:

SOMETHING FROM THE WEEK YOU WANT TO DISCONTINUE:

EMOTION TRACKING: HOW ARE YOU FEELING RIGHT NOW?

YOU CANNOT PROTECT YOURSELF
FROM SADNESS WITHOUT
PROTECTING YOURSELF FROM
HAPPINESS.

-JONATHAN SAFRAN FOER

WEEK OF:

WEEKLY SELF-CARE

PHYSICAL
(BODY)

INTELLECTUAL
(MIND)

PRACTICAL SELF-CARE:

SPIRITUAL
(CENTERED)

EMOTIONAL
(BALANCED)

SOMETHING NEW TO TRY:

TWO GOALS:

ONE BOUNDARY:

AN ANTICIPATED STRUGGLE THIS WEEK

STRUGGLE	ALL POTENTIAL SOLUTIONS	SOLUTION TO TRY

AN IMPROVEMENT FROM LAST WEEK

EMOTION TRACKING:
HOW ARE YOU FEELING RIGHT NOW?

FREE YOUR MIND

This page is for a brain dump. Note anything you have on your mind, make doodles, sketches, or Sketchnotes. Use it to organize your thoughts and empty your brain to make space.

WEEKLY JOURNAL

Optional Journal Prompt: Describe a day in your life that you would choose to relive. What made that day different? What made it special? Can you feel the emotions of that day as you write?

GRATITUDE JOURNAL

Each day write something that you are grateful for. As you write it, sink into the feeling you get when you think of it. Close your eyes. Allow the feeling to fill you up from your head to your toes.

MONDAY

TUESDAY

WEDNESDAY

THURSDAY

FRIDAY

SATURDAY

SUNDAY

NEW MINDFULNESS PRACTICE: BODY SCANS

Body scans are a systemic way of recognizing and reconnecting with feelings within your own body. Benefits of body scans are:

- "Enhances your ability to bring your full attention to real-time experiences happening in the present moment—helpful when emotions or thoughts feel wild.
- Trains to explore and be with pleasant and unpleasant sensations, learning to notice what happens when we simply hang in there and feel what's going on in "body-land" without trying to fix or change anything." (Smookler, Mindful.com)

It's recommended to use 30 minutes for this practice but can be done in 10 if necessary. You can also sit up instead of lying down if falling asleep is an issue.

TIP: Closing your eyes can be helpful to allow you to focus.

1. Bring your awareness to your body. You can systematically begin at the feet and work your way up or just go to where you feel sensations. Notice any feelings or pressure. When you're ready to move on, take a deep breath and more your attention to the next spot. Do so without judgment. Simply notice the feeling and bring awareness.
2. You may feel heat or cold, tingling, tightness, or a variety of other sensations.
3. If your attention wanders (and it probably will) simply and gently pull it back to the present moment. The more you practice the longer you will be able to work in this method.
4. When you've finished, open your eyes and gently begin to move your body.

There is no right way to do this which means there's also no wrong way. Do what feels comfortable and re-connect with your body.

MINDFULNESS PLAN & REFLECTION

Create a mindfulness plan for the week. Are there mindfulness activities that you know work for you? Is there something you would like to try? As you complete each day, focus on how it made you feel. Try not to think about HOW it went. Remember, a key ingredient to mindfulness is "without judgment."

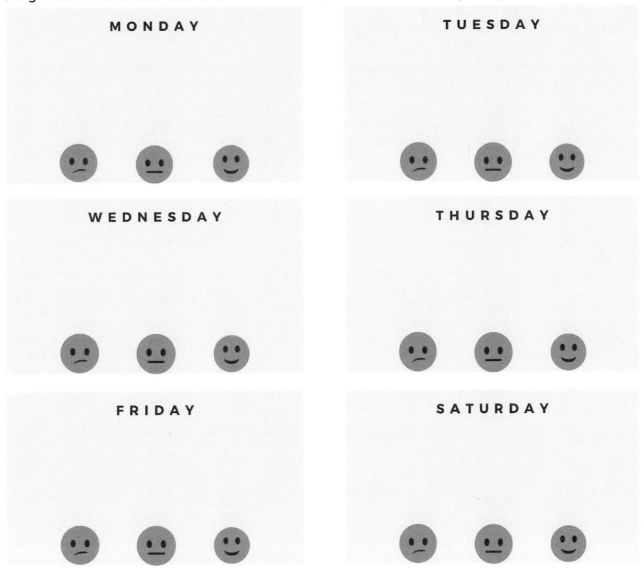

MONDAY

TUESDAY

WEDNESDAY

THURSDAY

FRIDAY

SATURDAY

SUNDAY

EDUCATOR ACTIVITY: WHAT ARE YOUR PASSIONS?

What are you passionate about personally? What are you passionate about professionally? Do these ever overlap? Where can you find places to incorporate your personal passions? How can you build on your professional passions? If you're not sure, how can you discover what they are?

If you are passionate about a topic or concept you are more likely to be engaged in the process. However, if you're going to school every day going through the motions it can lead to disengagement. Finding places where your passions meet your profession cohesively is one way to engage.

WEEKLY WRAP-UP

This page is about reflection. Reflect in whichever way makes the most sense to you. Maybe you write sentences, make notes, or draw. The purpose is to think about how your week went, any triggers you notice, or activities that went well.

YOUR OVERALL IMPRESSION OF THE WEEK

REFLECTION ON TWO GOALS

REFLECTION ON BOUNDARIES

REFLECTION ON YOUR ANTICIPATED STRUGGLE/SOLUTION:

SOMETHING FROM THE WEEK THAT MADE YOU HAPPY:

SOMETHING FROM THE WEEK YOU WANT TO DISCONTINUE:

EMOTION TRACKING: HOW ARE YOU FEELING RIGHT NOW?

*BENEFITS OF MEDITATION:

Reduces anxiety & stress

Promotes improves self-image &
a positive outlook

Lengthens attention span

May reduce age-related
memory loss

Can promote kindness

May help fight addiction

Improves sleep

Can decrease blood pressure

*Adapted from Healthline's 12 Science-Based Benefits of Meditation

WEEK OF:

WEEKLY SELF-CARE

PHYSICAL
(BODY)

INTELLECTUAL
(MIND)

PRACTICAL SELF-CARE:

SPIRITUAL
(CENTERED)

EMOTIONAL
(BALANCED)

SOMETHING NEW TO TRY:

TWO GOALS:

ONE BOUNDARY:

AN ANTICIPATED STRUGGLE THIS WEEK

STRUGGLE

ALL POTENTIAL SOLUTIONS

SOLUTION TO TRY

AN IMPROVEMENT FROM LAST WEEK

EMOTION TRACKING:
HOW ARE YOU FEELING RIGHT NOW?

FREE YOUR MIND

This page is for a brain dump. Note anything you have on your mind, make doodles, sketches, or Sketchnotes. Use it to organize your thoughts and empty your brain to make space.

WEEKLY JOURNAL

Optional Journal Prompt: You've been granted the power to go back in time to one particular day and "heal yourself". It could be physically, emotionally, spiritually...whatever. What would you do and why? How would your life be different with that healing?

_____
_____
_____
_____
_____
_____
_____
_____
_____
_____
_____
_____
_____
_____
_____
_____
_____
_____
_____
_____
_____
_____
_____
_____

NEW RESILIENCE PRACTICE: DEVELOP STRONG RELATIONSHIPS

Strong personal and professional relationships increase resilience. This isn't only because we have a support system when we need it, but also because our brains are wired to be social creatures. When we need help, we look to others around us for how to handle situations and for emotional support.

Sometimes, people find that they have better personal relationships than professional or vice versa. We need to be intentional about cultivating and maintaining important relationships in our lives so we have people who will hold us up when we feel like we are struggling to hold ourselves.

Think of three people in your personal life and three people in your professional life that you could do a better job at maintaining or creating a relationship.

Make a clear plan on how you will craft opportunities for connecting with those people in a more intentional way. Maybe you'll ask them for coffee. Maybe you'll open up to them more. Maybe you'll ask them to mentor you. Whatever the plan is, write it down and follow through.

Use the space below to write your plans. Include a date in which you'll complete the task for each person.

GRATITUDE JOURNAL

Each day write something that you are grateful for.
As you write it, sink into the feeling you get when
you think of it. Close your eyes. Allow the feeling to
fill you up from your head to your toes.

MONDAY

TUESDAY

WEDNESDAY

THURSDAY

FRIDAY

SATURDAY

SUNDAY

MINDFULNESS PLAN & REFLECTION

Create a mindfulness plan for the week. Are there mindfulness activities that you know work for you? Is there something you would like to try? As you complete each day, focus on how it made you feel. Try not to think about HOW it went. Remember, a key ingredient to mindfulness is "without judgment."

MONDAY

TUESDAY

WEDNESDAY

THURSDAY

FRIDAY

SATURDAY

SUNDAY

EDUCATOR ACTIVITY: WHAT ARE YOUR CORE BELIEFS?

Core beliefs are part of what tether us to education. They hold us up to standards and values that we set. When making decisions, we use core beliefs to help guide our answers.

What are your core beliefs? What do you truly believe about education? How it should function? Try to think of at least five of your core beliefs about education. Try to make them deeper than "everything we do should have the student in mind." This week, just develop the beliefs. Next week we will dive deeper.

Examples of core beliefs might be:
- All students can learn.
- A focus on teacher mental health is imperative.
- We should model the behaviors we wish to see.
- Professional learning is an opportunity to grow.

What are yours?

_____

_____

_____

_____

_____

_____

_____

_____

_____

_____

_____

_____

_____

_____

WEEKLY WRAP-UP

This page is about reflection. Reflect in whichever way makes the most sense to you. Maybe you write sentences, make notes, or draw. The purpose is to think about how your week went, any triggers you notice, or activities that went well.

YOUR OVERALL IMPRESSION OF THE WEEK

REFLECTION ON TWO GOALS

REFLECTION ON BOUNDARIES

REFLECTION ON YOUR ANTICIPATED STRUGGLE/SOLUTION:

SOMETHING FROM THE WEEK THAT MADE YOU HAPPY:

SOMETHING FROM THE WEEK YOU WANT TO DISCONTINUE:

EMOTION TRACKING:
HOW ARE YOU FEELING RIGHT NOW?

REIKI

Reiki is energy healing - like chiropractic care for your energy. You may be most familiar with it as what Mr. Miyagi did for Daniel in the Karate Kid when he'd rub his hands together. Reiki practitioners use guidance and energy to clear and heal physical, emotional, spiritual, and energetic issues in the body.

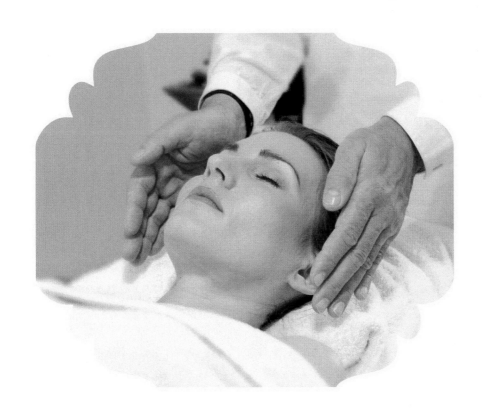

WEEK OF:

WEEKLY SELF-CARE

PHYSICAL (BODY)	INTELLECTUAL (MIND)	PRACTICAL SELF-CARE:

SPIRITUAL (CENTERED)	EMOTIONAL (BALANCED)	SOMETHING NEW TO TRY:

TWO GOALS:

ONE BOUNDARY:

AN ANTICIPATED STRUGGLE THIS WEEK

STRUGGLE	ALL POTENTIAL SOLUTIONS	SOLUTION TO TRY

AN IMPROVEMENT FROM LAST WEEK

EMOTION TRACKING:
HOW ARE YOU FEELING RIGHT NOW?

FREE YOUR MIND

This page is for a brain dump. Note anything you have on your mind, make doodles, sketches, or Sketchnotes. Use it to organize your thoughts and empty your brain to make space.

WEEKLY JOURNAL

Optional Journal Prompt: A popular quote from Harry Potter is: "Happiness can be found in the darkest of times if only one remembers to turn on the light." - Albus Dumbledore. What does this quote mean to you? Do you agree?

NEW RESILIENCE PRACTICE: MANTRAS

A mantra is an inspiring, positive saying, prayer, or chant that is repeated. It is generally used to aid in mindfulness. It is one of the ways to exercise the mindfulness muscle, however, in creating this practice and making positive connections in your brain, you're also practicing resilience.

Examples of mantras are:

- When I breathe in, I send myself love.
- Love every minute of life.
- Expect nothing and appreciate everything.

The steps to practicing mantras are:

1. Choose or write the mantra you'd like to use.
2. Memorize it.
3. Write it 10 times with your non-dominate hand.
4. Notice any difficult feelings while you're doing it. Does it make you uncomfortable? Usually, these feelings show up in your gut. Doing it legibly with your non writing hand forces you to stay in the moment as you're practicing.

Use the space below for your first mantra practice.

GRATITUDE JOURNAL

Each day write something that you are grateful for.
As you write it, sink into the feeling you get when
you think of it. Close your eyes. Allow the feeling to
fill you up from your head to your toes.

MONDAY

TUESDAY

WEDNESDAY

THURSDAY

FRIDAY

SATURDAY

SUNDAY

NEW MINDFULNESS PRACTICE: MINDFUL EATING

We are so busy nowadays that we barely sit and have a meal anymore without being involved in some other activity at the same time. We don't pay attention to our eating so we eat until we are overly full and don't even taste our food. Mindful eating is an exercise to bring you back to your meal and be aware of your senses and the meal you have in front of you. Mindful eating pulls you away from mindlessly eating things and instead focuses on the food and how it makes you feel.

The Raisin Exercise is a common tool for teaching mindful eating. It is also a fun activity to introduce mindfulness to students.

Raisin Exercise:

1. Hold a raisin in your fingers.
2. Be completely absorbed in the raisin.
3. Look at the raisin and notice what it looks like.
4. Rub your fingers over the raisin. How does it feel?
5. Smell the raisin. Does it have a particular scent?
6. Put the raisin on your tongue. Become completely absorbed in how the raisin feels on your tongue.
7. Shift it to a different part of your mouth. What do you notice is different about it in the new place? Notice with no judgment.
8. Slowly bite down and notice how the raisin feels and tastes. Resist the urge to swallow. Move it. Notice how sweet it tastes.
9. Swallow the raisin while you notice how the raisin goes down your throat.

Reflection: What was difference from the experience from the last time you ate a raisin? How would mindfully eating change the way you approach meals?

MINDFULNESS PLAN & REFLECTION

Create a mindfulness plan for the week. Are there mindfulness activities that you know work for you? Is there something you would like to try? As you complete each day, focus on how it made you feel. Try not to think about HOW it went. Remember, a key ingredient to mindfulness is "without judgment."

MONDAY

TUESDAY

WEDNESDAY

THURSDAY

FRIDAY

SATURDAY

SUNDAY

EDUCATOR ACTIVITY: CORE BELIEFS PART DEUX

Last week you wrote down your core beliefs about education. You were also told that your core beliefs are what tether you to education.

Look back at the core beliefs you wrote down. Go through each one and reflect on these questions:

How do you live those core beliefs in your everyday work?

What, if anything, holds you back from believing that you are fully functioning within your core beliefs?

How can you function within those core beliefs EVEN IF there are constraints that feel like they are working against you?

If your core beliefs tether you to education, it's important to find ways to live those everyday to keep you engaged despite the constraints that may be holding you back.

_____

_____

_____

_____

_____

_____

_____

_____

_____

_____

_____

_____

WEEKLY WRAP-UP

This page is about reflection. Reflect in whichever way makes the most sense to you. Maybe you write sentences, make notes, or draw. The purpose is to think about how your week went, any triggers you notice, or activities that went well.

YOUR OVERALL IMPRESSION OF THE WEEK

REFLECTION ON TWO GOALS

REFLECTION ON BOUNDARIES

REFLECTION ON YOUR ANTICIPATED STRUGGLE/SOLUTION:

SOMETHING FROM THE WEEK THAT MADE YOU HAPPY:

SOMETHING FROM THE WEEK YOU WANT TO DISCONTINUE:

EMOTION TRACKING:
HOW ARE YOU FEELING RIGHT NOW?

FIVE GUIDELINES FOR SELF-CARE

SELF-CARE FEELS GOOD AND MAKES YOU HAPPY

FOCUS ON POSITIVE SELF-TALK

AVOID DRAMA AND NEGATIVITY

LET GO OF WHAT YOU CAN'T CONTROL; FOCUS ON WHAT YOU CAN

KNOW WHEN TO SAY NO AND BE EXCITED ABOUT SAYING YES

WEEK OF:

WEEKLY SELF-CARE

PHYSICAL (BODY)	INTELLECTUAL (MIND)	PRACTICAL SELF-CARE:
SPIRITUAL (CENTERED)	EMOTIONAL (BALANCED)	SOMETHING NEW TO TRY:

TWO GOALS:

ONE BOUNDARY:

AN ANTICIPATED STRUGGLE THIS WEEK

STRUGGLE	ALL POTENTIAL SOLUTIONS	SOLUTION TO TRY

AN IMPROVEMENT FROM LAST WEEK

EMOTION TRACKING:
HOW ARE YOU FEELING RIGHT NOW?

FREE YOUR MIND

This page is for a brain dump. Note anything you have on your mind, make doodles, sketches, or Sketchnotes. Use it to organize your thoughts and empty your brain to make space.

WEEKLY JOURNAL

Optional Journal Prompt: Reflect on how you have changed since five years ago.

_____
_____
_____
_____
_____
_____
_____
_____
_____
_____
_____
_____
_____
_____
_____
_____
_____
_____
_____
_____
_____
_____

NEW GRATITUDE PRACTICE:
FIVE QUICK TEXTS

In appreciating our neighbor, we're
participating in something truly sacred.
~ Fred Rogers

The idea behind five quick texts is simple...to send five texts to five people telling them you appreciate them or you're thinking about them. This could be done over the course of the week one at a time or all five it once. If you don't have the ability to text, think about dropping a note in the mail or leaving post-it notes on co-workers desks.

Whether you're texting to show appreciation or that you're thinking about them, it should be personal and specific. Also, as you type the text in, feel the emotion that comes with thinking about that person. Imagine you're sending it along with the text.

For example, instead of sending "I just wanted you to know I'm grateful for you" think about sending "I wanted to know that I appreciate the way you make me laugh when I really need it."

This gratitude practice is the emotional equivalent of a "pay it forward" gift. You cause someone else to feel positive emotion as you practice your gratitude.

You could use the space below to keep track of who you sent texts to in case you'd like to try it again with different people.

GRATITUDE JOURNAL

Each day write something that you are grateful for. As you write it, sink into the feeling you get when you think of it. Close your eyes. Allow the feeling to fill you up from your head to your toes.

MONDAY

TUESDAY

WEDNESDAY

THURSDAY

FRIDAY

SATURDAY

SUNDAY

MINDFULNESS PLAN & REFLECTION

Create a mindfulness plan for the week. Are there mindfulness activities that you know work for you? Is there something you would like to try? As you complete each day, focus on how it made you feel. Try not to think about HOW it went. Remember, a key ingredient to mindfulness is "without judgment."

MONDAY

TUESDAY

WEDNESDAY

THURSDAY

FRIDAY

SATURDAY

SUNDAY

EDUCATOR ACTIVITY:
YOUR PURPOSE IN EDUCATION

At this point you've written your core beliefs, you've determined how you live them, you have potentially even gone back and rewrote them after you processed a little more. If you truly decide to hold your core beliefs as sacred, you will continually. go through this molding process. Some beliefs may never change while others may go through slight revisions. You may add some on as you learn and grow.

Your core beliefs should support your purpose. Once you know your purpose, it strengthens the tethers that the core beliefs already provide because you know why you're there. Write down what you think your purpose is. Try to be more specific than "to help students learn". What special characteristics, strengths, and knowledge do you bring to the profession to enhance it? Finally, does your purpose act as an umbrella to include all your core beliefs?

_____

_____

_____

_____

_____

_____

_____

_____

_____

_____

_____

_____

WEEKLY WRAP-UP

This page is about reflection. Reflect in whichever way makes the most sense to you. Maybe you write sentences, make notes, or draw. The purpose is to think about how your week went, any triggers you notice, or activities that went well.

YOUR OVERALL IMPRESSION OF THE WEEK

REFLECTION ON TWO GOALS

REFLECTION ON BOUNDARIES

REFLECTION ON YOUR ANTICIPATED STRUGGLE/SOLUTION:

SOMETHING FROM THE WEEK THAT MADE YOU HAPPY:

SOMETHING FROM THE WEEK YOU WANT TO DISCONTINUE:

EMOTION TRACKING:
HOW ARE YOU FEELING RIGHT NOW?

Breathe

LET GO

AND REMIND YOURSELF THAT THIS IS THE ONLY MOMENT THAT YOU KNOW YOU HAVE FOR SURE.

-OPRAH WINFREY

WEEK OF:

WEEKLY SELF-CARE

PHYSICAL (BODY)	INTELLECTUAL (MIND)	PRACTICAL SELF-CARE:

SPIRITUAL (CENTERED)	EMOTIONAL (BALANCED)	SOMETHING NEW TO TRY:

TWO GOALS:

ONE BOUNDARY:

AN ANTICIPATED STRUGGLE THIS WEEK

STRUGGLE	ALL POTENTIAL SOLUTIONS	SOLUTION TO TRY

AN IMPROVEMENT FROM LAST WEEK

EMOTION TRACKING:
HOW ARE YOU FEELING RIGHT NOW?

FREE YOUR MIND

This page is for a brain dump. Note anything you have on your mind, make doodles, sketches, or Sketchnotes. Use it to organize your thoughts and empty your brain to make space.

WEEKLY JOURNAL

Optional Journal Prompt: Recall a defining moment in your personal or professional life. What was it? Why do you consider it to be pivotal?

_____

_____

_____

_____

_____

_____

_____

_____

_____

_____

_____

_____

_____

_____

_____

_____

_____

_____

_____

_____

_____

_____

GRATITUDE JOURNAL

Each day write something that you are grateful for. As you write it, sink into the feeling you get when you think of it. Close your eyes. Allow the feeling to fill you up from your head to your toes.

MONDAY

TUESDAY

WEDNESDAY

THURSDAY

FRIDAY

SATURDAY

SUNDAY

NEW MINDFULNESS PRACTICE: SENSES EXERCISE

This exercise is a quick and effective way to ground yourself back in the present. If you find yourself future forecasting, ruminating on negativity, or feeling anxiety focusing on your five senses in the moment can break you of that cycle.

Find a comfortable place to sit with your feet on the ground. Bring your awareness and attention into the moment. You can focus on each of the senses anywhere from 10 seconds to one minute. Whatever feels comfortable. If your attention at any point starts to waiver, gently bring it back.

Start with sight. Notice something in the room that you haven't noticed before. If this isn't possible, then notice an object and something different about it (shadow, the way the light is hitting on the object). Keep looking at it for your chosen length of time.

Sound. Maintain all focus on any sound you can hear. One sound, exclusively focus on that sound.

Touch. Engage your sense of touch. Grab an object and observe it with a beginners eye but from the sense of touch. Feel it. Could be something soft or have a texture. What does it feel like? Be attentive to the actual sensation of holding the object.

Smell. Is there a smell in the air? If there's nothing apparent you can smell, are you wearing lotion or perfume? Can you smell yourself?

Taste. Engage the sense of taste and hold your awareness on something you can taste. If you have food or drink around you can do this, but you can also just notice the taste of your own saliva or teeth.

MINDFULNESS PLAN & REFLECTION

Create a mindfulness plan for the week. Are there mindfulness activities that you know work for you? Is there something you would like to try? As you complete each day, focus on how it made you feel. Try not to think about HOW it went. Remember, a key ingredient to mindfulness is "without judgment."

MONDAY

TUESDAY

WEDNESDAY

THURSDAY

FRIDAY

SATURDAY

SUNDAY

EDUCATOR ACTIVITY: PERSONALIZING PROFESSIONAL LEARNING

Whether you feel like your district gives you all the amazing professional learning opportunities that you could need or they give you none, professional learning needs to be driven by an educator for themselves. Professional learning is important not only because.it helps you grow, but it can also keep you engaged by speaking to your professional passions and/or keeping your anxiety down by helping you understand how to do certain aspects of your job.

The reality is that there aren't many, if any, districts that can give each individual teacher everything they need at any given time. Therefore, like our students, we need to be responsible for our own learning to truly meet our potential.

Reflect on some areas that you would like professional learning and write a quick plan on how you will seek opportunities. Books? Social media? Online courses? Asking your district? Brainstorm practical ways you could work on these areas.

A PASSION AREA

SOMETHING BRAND NEW

AN AREA OF STRENGTH TO BUILD ON

AN AREA OF IN NEED OF GROWTH

WEEKLY WRAP-UP

This page is about reflection. Reflect in whichever way makes the most sense to you. Maybe you write sentences, make notes, or draw. The purpose is to think about how your week went, any triggers you notice, or activities that went well.

YOUR OVERALL IMPRESSION OF THE WEEK

REFLECTION ON TWO GOALS

REFLECTION ON BOUNDARIES

REFLECTION ON YOUR ANTICIPATED STRUGGLE/SOLUTION:

SOMETHING FROM THE WEEK THAT MADE YOU HAPPY:

SOMETHING FROM THE WEEK YOU WANT TO DISCONTINUE:

EMOTION TRACKING:
HOW ARE YOU FEELING RIGHT NOW?

LOVE AND LIGHT ARE THE ROOT OF ALL HEALING. WHY DO YOU DENY SUCH GREATNESS?

THERE MAY BE CHALLENGES BUT NOTHING SO GREAT THAT IT IS INSURMOUNTABLE.

LOVE IS THE ULTIMATE RESOURCE. BASK IN IT. GIVE IT TO OTHERS.

NOTHING IS MORE IMPORTANT.

WEEK OF:

WEEKLY SELF-CARE

| PHYSICAL (BODY) | INTELLECTUAL (MIND) | PRACTICAL SELF-CARE: |
| SPIRITUAL (CENTERED) | EMOTIONAL (BALANCED) | SOMETHING NEW TO TRY: |

TWO GOALS:

ONE BOUNDARY:

AN ANTICIPATED STRUGGLE THIS WEEK

| STRUGGLE | ALL POTENTIAL SOLUTIONS | SOLUTION TO TRY |

AN IMPROVEMENT FROM LAST WEEK

EMOTION TRACKING:
HOW ARE YOU FEELING RIGHT NOW?

FREE YOUR MIND

This page is for a brain dump. Note anything you have on your mind, make doodles, sketches, or Sketchnotes. Use it to organize your thoughts and empty your brain to make space.

WEEKLY JOURNAL

Optional Journal Prompt: What has happened in a day when you can come home and say, "I had a really great day today."

_____

_____

_____

_____

_____

_____

_____

_____

_____

_____

_____

_____

_____

_____

_____

_____

_____

_____

_____

_____

_____

_____

NEW GRATITUDE PRACTICE: COUNT YOUR BLESSINGS

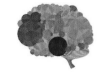

You've heard the term "count your blessings" but have you ever really? What if you had to write down 20 of them? 50? 100? Would you be able to do it?

This gratitude challenge is about recognizing everything in your life - past and present - that you're grateful for. All the experiences, people, and opportunities, good and bad, that you feel appreciation. It's not a competition to have more than anyone else or a challenge to get a certain number. It's about being able to look at your list and see, in writing, a long list of blessings. Use the rest of this page for this practice.

GRATITUDE JOURNAL

Each day write something that you are grateful for. As you write it, sink into the feeling you get when you think of it. Close your eyes. Allow the feeling to fill you up from your head to your toes.

MONDAY

TUESDAY

WEDNESDAY

THURSDAY

FRIDAY

SATURDAY

SUNDAY

MINDFULNESS PLAN & REFLECTION

Create a mindfulness plan for the week. Are there mindfulness activities that you know work for you? Is there something you would like to try? As you complete each day, focus on how it made you feel. Try not to think about HOW it went. Remember, a key ingredient to mindfulness is "without judgment."

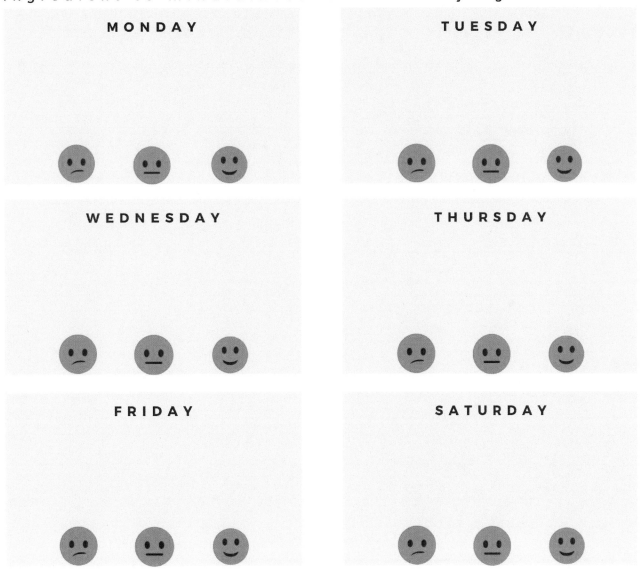

MONDAY

TUESDAY

WEDNESDAY

THURSDAY

FRIDAY

SATURDAY

SUNDAY

EDUCATOR ACTIVITY:
FIND THE HUMOR

Think back across your career. Whether that career has been one year or 20 years, guaranteed you have had some moments where you laughed with students, they said something funny, or they touched your heart. Relive those moments. Write them down. If you like, keep this page in a place where you can pull it out and reread it during difficult times. These are some of the moments that tie us to education.

_____

_____

_____

_____

_____

_____

_____

_____

_____

_____

_____

_____

_____

_____

_____

_____

_____

_____

_____

_____

WEEKLY WRAP-UP

This page is about reflection. Reflect in whichever way makes the most sense to you. Maybe you write sentences, make notes, or draw. The purpose is to think about how your week went, any triggers you notice, or activities that went well.

YOUR OVERALL IMPRESSION OF THE WEEK

REFLECTION ON TWO GOALS

REFLECTION ON BOUNDARIES

REFLECTION ON YOUR ANTICIPATED STRUGGLE/SOLUTION:

SOMETHING FROM THE WEEK THAT MADE YOU HAPPY:

SOMETHING FROM THE WEEK YOU WANT TO DISCONTINUE:

EMOTION TRACKING: HOW ARE YOU FEELING RIGHT NOW?

TAKING A DEEP BREATH HELPS YOU MOVE OUT OF YOUR SYMPATHETIC NERVOUS SYSTEM (FIGHT OR FLIGHT) TO YOUR PARASYMPATHETIC NERVOUS SYSTEM (RELAX).

THE BREATH LITERALLY TELLS YOUR BODY TO RELAX.

THIS IS ESPECIALLY HELPFUL IF YOU PRACTICE CONSCIOUS BREATHING TECHNIQUES, WHERE YOU ARE MORE MINDFUL OF HOW YOU ARE BREATHING.

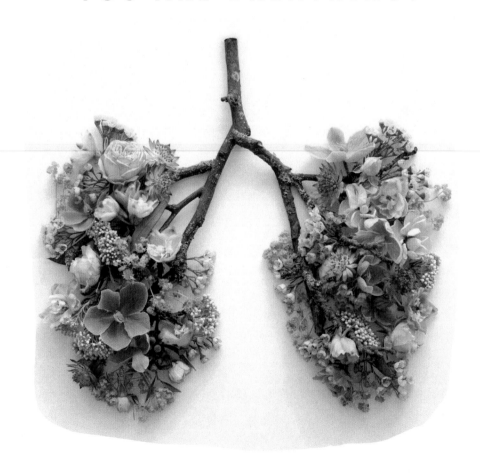

WEEK OF:

WEEKLY SELF-CARE

PHYSICAL (BODY)	INTELLECTUAL (MIND)	PRACTICAL SELF-CARE:

SPIRITUAL (CENTERED)	EMOTIONAL (BALANCED)	SOMETHING NEW TO TRY:

TWO GOALS:

ONE BOUNDARY:

AN ANTICIPATED STRUGGLE THIS WEEK

STRUGGLE	ALL POTENTIAL SOLUTIONS	SOLUTION TO TRY

AN IMPROVEMENT FROM LAST WEEK

EMOTION TRACKING:
HOW ARE YOU FEELING RIGHT NOW?

FREE YOUR MIND

This page is for a brain dump. Note anything you have on your mind, make doodles, sketches, or Sketchnotes. Use it to organize your thoughts and empty your brain to make space.

WEEKLY JOURNAL

Optional Journal Prompt: We work with people every day and yet it isn't often that people get to see our true selves. What is one thing you wish people knew about you? How would it change your interactions if they did?

_____

_____

_____

_____

_____

_____

_____

_____

_____

_____

_____

_____

_____

_____

_____

_____

_____

_____

_____

_____

_____

_____

_____

GRATITUDE JOURNAL

Each day write something that you are grateful for. As you write it, sink into the feeling you get when you think of it. Close your eyes. Allow the feeling to fill you up from your head to your toes.

MONDAY

TUESDAY

WEDNESDAY

THURSDAY

FRIDAY

SATURDAY

SUNDAY

NEW MINDFULNESS PRACTICE: CONSCIOUS BREATHING

Conscious breathing is learning how to breathe correctly in order to help your body work the way it's supposed to. Many times, people find that when they are stressed or worried they breathe shallow. This can impact everything from the oxygen that is going to your brain to the way your tongue and jaw function if you are constantly breathing through your mouth. Being aware of your breathing is a part of conscious breathing, but is really just the tip of the iceberg. I highly recommend doing more research into conscious breathing if you find that you too may have been practicing breathing wrong your whole life.

An easy beginning breathing exercise is called Coherent Breathing and goes like this:

Find a quiet place to sit. Set your timer for five minutes. Relax your body and your jaw.

1. Practice breathing by inhaling for five seconds. Notice the air going through your nose and into your chest and belly.
2. Without pausing, exhale for five seconds. Notice the air leaving your belly, lungs, and then your nose.
3. Take deep, purposeful breaths for five minutes.

What do you notice about how you feel as you finish? Was it a difficult practice to slowly breath in and out? Could you do it for the entire five minutes? You may need to practice multiple times to be able to complete the exercise and feel the impact of conscious breathing.

MINDFULNESS PLAN & REFLECTION

Create a mindfulness plan for the week. Are there
mindfulness activities that you know work for you? Is
there something you would like to try? As you
complete each day, focus on how it made you feel.
Try not to think about HOW it went. Remember, a key
ingredient to mindfulness is "without judgment."

MONDAY

TUESDAY

WEDNESDAY

THURSDAY

FRIDAY

SATURDAY

SUNDAY

EDUCATOR ACTIVITY: SHARING YOUR KNOWLEDGE

Creating connections with others is one of the ways to get or stay engaged. A valuable practice for making connections is sharing your knowledge. EVERYONE HAS SOMETHING TO SHARE WITH OTHERS. There is a practice, a unit, a lesson, a foundational belief, a core belief, and/or a purpose that others want to hear about. How can you share your knowledge with others? Would you like to try social media? A blog? A presentation for your staff or at a conference? Choose a way to create professional connections by sharing your knowledge. Then, create a practical plan for moving forward.

ONE OF MY MANY GIFTS I'D LIKE TO SHARE

MY PLAN FOR SHARING

WEEKLY WRAP-UP

This page is about reflection. Reflect in whichever way makes the most sense to you. Maybe you write sentences, make notes, or draw. The purpose is to think about how your week went, any triggers you notice, or activities that went well.

YOUR OVERALL IMPRESSION OF THE WEEK

REFLECTION ON TWO GOALS

REFLECTION ON BOUNDARIES

REFLECTION ON YOUR ANTICIPATED STRUGGLE/SOLUTION:

SOMETHING FROM THE WEEK THAT MADE YOU HAPPY:

SOMETHING FROM THE WEEK YOU WANT TO DISCONTINUE:

EMOTION TRACKING:
HOW ARE YOU FEELING RIGHT NOW?

OWNING OUR STORY
AND LOVING OURSELVES
THROUGH THAT PROCESS IS
THE BRAVEST THING THAT
WE'LL EVER DO.

-BRENE BROWN

WEEK OF:

WEEKLY SELF-CARE

PHYSICAL (BODY)	INTELLECTUAL (MIND)	PRACTICAL SELF-CARE:
SPIRITUAL (CENTERED)	EMOTIONAL (BALANCED)	SOMETHING NEW TO TRY:

TWO GOALS:

ONE BOUNDARY:

AN ANTICIPATED STRUGGLE THIS WEEK

STRUGGLE	ALL POTENTIAL SOLUTIONS	SOLUTION TO TRY

AN IMPROVEMENT FROM LAST WEEK

EMOTION TRACKING:
HOW ARE YOU FEELING RIGHT NOW?

FREE YOUR MIND

This page is for a brain dump. Note anything you have on your mind, make doodles, sketches, or Sketchnotes. Use it to organize your thoughts and empty your brain to make space.

WEEKLY JOURNAL

Optional Journal Prompt: What does it mean to live an authentic life?

_____

_____

_____

_____

_____

_____

_____

_____

_____

_____

_____

_____

_____

_____

_____

_____

_____

_____

_____

_____

_____

_____

_____

NEW RESILIENCE PRACTICE: WHAT BRINGS YOU JOY

A baby's birth, an engagement, a wedding, a holiday...these are all large ticket items that could bring you joy. But, what about the every day? What about finding joy in-between large celebrations?

One way to build resilience is to find joys in the every day, and to do that you need to know what they are. What little, daily activities or happenings catch your attention? Take your breath away? Make you stop and enjoy the moment?

It could be the sunrise or sunset, the city skyline, or an apple tree full of fruit. To best be able to recognize these little joyful moments we need to know what brings us joy. Below, think of a few every day (or every so often) occurrences that fill you with joy. The point is to recognize the feeling they bring you and allow that to fill you up. Not only is it a way to enjoy life more, but it also helps us in times of adversity as it becomes more of a habit to recognize these things.

GRATITUDE JOURNAL

Each day write something that you are grateful for. As you write it, sink into the feeling you get when you think of it. Close your eyes. Allow the feeling to fill you up from your head to your toes.

MONDAY

TUESDAY

WEDNESDAY

THURSDAY

FRIDAY

SATURDAY

SUNDAY

MINDFULNESS PLAN & REFLECTION

Create a mindfulness plan for the week. Are there mindfulness activities that you know work for you? Is there something you would like to try? As you complete each day, focus on how it made you feel. Try not to think about HOW it went. Remember, a key ingredient to mindfulness is "without judgment."

MONDAY

TUESDAY

WEDNESDAY

THURSDAY

FRIDAY

SATURDAY

SUNDAY

EDUCATOR ACTIVITY: SELF CARE IN THE CLASSROOM

There are times in a classroom when you need quick self-care options that won't throw off your day but will at the very least keep your emotions in check and healthy. Here are some suggestions.

Take a deep breath: Remember, taking a deep breath literally tells your body to relax. When I would take a deep breath as a teacher, I would couple it with a drink of coffee or water or put candy in my mouth (that was similar enough to a cough drop that I could pass it off). The extra couple seconds I'd get while doing this gave me a moment to focus on my heart rate and breath.

Have your Joy Kit ready: Remember from earlier weeks, joy kits are first aid kits for when you need to feel happy. They can be in a small box in your desk and should be filled with small items or photographs that bring you joy. Take something out of the joy kit, put it in your hand, look at it, close your eyes, and allow the feeling it gives you to fill you up. It can only take a minute or two but should provide a feeling of calm before you head back into the trenches.

Involve the students. Have the students take a break: In the scenario above, the students taking a break to regroup and focus back on learning would have been best suited before the directions were given when the teacher knew she/he was losing them. Taking a break to run through a few easy yoga poses, deep breathing, or even coloring a picture (yes, for secondary, too) for a few minutes are all proven ways to get the brain ready to learn. As for the teacher...either using this time to practice along with them or taking a few minutes to look at the joy kit will help get them back on track as well.

A little planning can go a long way when the minutes count. Understanding what works for you is the first step. Understanding the little things that give you joy is the second step. That takes pre-planning but is very important information to have when you're practicing self-care.

WEEKLY WRAP-UP

This page is about reflection. Reflect in whichever way makes the most sense to you. Maybe you write sentences, make notes, or draw. The purpose is to think about how your week went, any triggers you notice, or activities that went well.

YOUR OVERALL IMPRESSION OF THE WEEK

REFLECTION ON TWO GOALS

REFLECTION ON BOUNDARIES

REFLECTION ON YOUR ANTICIPATED STRUGGLE/SOLUTION:

SOMETHING FROM THE WEEK THAT MADE YOU HAPPY:

SOMETHING FROM THE WEEK YOU WANT TO DISCONTINUE:

EMOTION TRACKING:
HOW ARE YOU FEELING RIGHT NOW?

KINTSUGI
IS THE JAPANESE ART OF
REPAIRING BROKEN PIECES
OF POTTERY WITH GOLD.
THE BELIEF IS THAT THE
HEALING ADDS TO THE
BEAUTY AND HISTORY OF
THE PIECE.

WEEK OF:

WEEKLY SELF-CARE

PHYSICAL (BODY)	**INTELLECTUAL** (MIND)	**PRACTICAL** **SELF-CARE:**
SPIRITUAL (CENTERED)	**EMOTIONAL** (BALANCED)	**SOMETHING NEW** **TO TRY:**

TWO GOALS:

ONE BOUNDARY:

AN ANTICIPATED STRUGGLE THIS WEEK

STRUGGLE	ALL POTENTIAL SOLUTIONS	SOLUTION TO TRY

AN IMPROVEMENT FROM LAST WEEK

EMOTION TRACKING:
HOW ARE YOU FEELING RIGHT NOW?

FREE YOUR MIND

This page is for a brain dump. Note anything you have on your mind, make doodles, sketches, or Sketchnotes. Use it to organize your thoughts and empty your brain to make space.

WEEKLY JOURNAL

Optional Journal Prompt: What would you do if you knew you could not fail?

_____
_____
_____
_____
_____
_____
_____
_____
_____
_____
_____
_____
_____
_____
_____
_____
_____
_____
_____
_____
_____
_____
_____

GRATITUDE JOURNAL

Each day write something that you are grateful for. As you write it, sink into the feeling you get when you think of it. Close your eyes. Allow the feeling to fill you up from your head to your toes.

MONDAY

TUESDAY

WEDNESDAY

THURSDAY

FRIDAY

SATURDAY

SUNDAY

NEW MINDFULNESS PRACTICE: MINDFUL WALKS

Mindful walking, similar to mindful breathing, may feel like something we do all the time and shouldn't necessarily be something we have to practice. However, when was the last time you took a walk and stayed in the moment? Or did you zone out and think about what happened earlier that week or what is about to happen next week? Many people go for hikes or walks, but not many people stay in the moment when they do it.

To practice mindful walking, pick a place to go for a walk. If you love to be in nature, you can practice here but it doesn't need to be done anywhere specific.

- Start out slow and create a goal for a short amount of time - maybe 10 minutes the first few times you practice.
- You will be reconditioning your focus to remain fully immersed in the experience.
- Notice your lower body and what it feels like to walk – as your heels hit the ground, the way your calves move, then to your upper body...how your breath changes.
- Notice what you feel with each of your senses. What do you hear? Smell?
- If your mind begins to wander, gently pull it back into the moment. If you have a difficult time maintaining focus create checkpoints. For example, "From this point on I am going to remain mindful of what I am experiencing." Use a visual cue to help - it could be mailboxes or stop signs for example. When you get to one checkpoint, create another to keep going.

Keep in mind you're trying to create new, healthy habits so if it doesn't go perfectly the first time, keep practicing. Reflect when you're finished...how do you feel after the mindful walk?

MINDFULNESS PLAN & REFLECTION

Create a mindfulness plan for the week. Are there mindfulness activities that you know work for you? Is there something you would like to try? As you complete each day, focus on how it made you feel. Try not to think about HOW it went. Remember, a key ingredient to mindfulness is "without judgment."

MONDAY

TUESDAY

WEDNESDAY

THURSDAY

FRIDAY

SATURDAY

SUNDAY

EDUCATOR ACTIVITY: THE PLAN FROM HERE

Staying engaged or re-engaging is a personal journey. It is a winding road where the only way to be happy is to grab happiness by the horns and take control of it. We are responsible for our own happiness and it is a choice we can make every day.

How are you going to continue taking control of your happiness moving forward? What can you continue to do to keep yourself accountable and working toward engagement?

_____

_____

_____

_____

_____

_____

_____

_____

_____

_____

_____

_____

_____

_____

_____

_____

_____

_____

WEEKLY WRAP-UP

This page is about reflection. Reflect in whichever way makes the most sense to you. Maybe you write sentences, make notes, or draw. The purpose is to think about how your week went, any triggers you notice, or activities that went well.

YOUR OVERALL IMPRESSION OF THE WEEK

REFLECTION ON TWO GOALS

REFLECTION ON BOUNDARIES

REFLECTION ON YOUR ANTICIPATED STRUGGLE/SOLUTION:

SOMETHING FROM THE WEEK THAT MADE YOU HAPPY:

SOMETHING FROM THE WEEK YOU WANT TO DISCONTINUE:

EMOTION TRACKING:
HOW ARE YOU FEELING RIGHT NOW?

Final Reflection and Moving Forward

It may be over, but this is just the beginning.

Look back through the book and pay special attention to the emotion tracking. Do you notice anything about triggers? Are there certain times of the week, month, or year that seem to be harder for you? Why do you think that is? Can you better prepare for them?

Read back through your educator reflections. What did you learn? Do you feel more tethered to your job? Are you at least beginning to feel that pull back to what you're doing? What are your next steps to keep moving forward? How can you include your family and professional community to support you on your journey?

DON'T STOP. This can't be the end. You'll need to continue these practices to heal and/or maintain the growth you've experienced.

If you've gone through this entire book faithfully this is what you've developed:
- 14 weeks of building healthy habits.
- Regular practices of gratitude and mindfulness.
- Deep reflective skills.
- The ability to be more proactive and ready for potential struggles, as well as developing a solutions mindset.
- Boundaries and at least the beginning stages of properly setting them by acknowledging what they are.
- Better and more well-rounded self-care routines.

That is a crazy amount to accomplish in 14 weeks! Take time to celebrate your win!

About the Author

Mandy Froehlich passionately encourages educators to create innovative change in their classrooms. A former Director of Innovation and Technology, technology integrator, and teacher, she has experience at many levels of the organizational structure. Currently, as a full-time education consultant, keynote speaker, and presenter, her interest lies in reinvigorating and re-engaging teachers back into their profession, educator mental health, social-emotional support, and mindfulness, as well as what's needed to support teachers in their pursuit of innovative and divergent thinking and teaching. She consults internationally with school districts and post-secondary institutions in the effective use of technology to support great teaching, mental health support for educators, and how to create organizational change. Her first book, *The Fire Within: Lessons from defeat that have ignited a passion for learning*, discusses mental health awareness for teachers. Her second book, *Divergent EDU*, is based on an organizational structure she developed to support teachers in innovative and divergent thinking. Her third book, *Reignite the Flames: Finding our passion and purpose for learning among the embers* discusses educator mental health and engagement and how to re-engage back into the profession. All of her books can be found on Amazon and Barnes and Noble in both digital and print formats.

Find Mandy at www.mandyfroehlich.com or on Twitter at @froehlichm. Also, find a link to her FREE educator self-care course on her website.

Want to bring Mandy to your school or organization? Contact her at mandyfroehlichedu@gmail.com or use the contact form on her website.

Additional Books by Mandy Froehlich

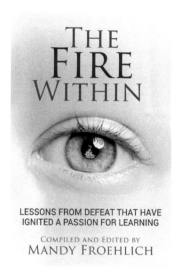

Adversity itself is not what defines us. It is how we react to that adversity and the choices we make that creates who we are and how we will persevere. ***The Fire Within: Lessons from defeat that have ignited a passion for learning*** is a compilation of stories from amazing educators who have faced personal adversity head on and have become stronger people for it. They use their new-found strength to support the students and teachers they work with. They are sharing their stories with a hope that others in the same situations might not feel alone, knowing that in our darkest hours, when our situations feel the most hopeless, is when we develop the extraordinary characteristics that make us who we are at our very cores. In addition to the powerful and inspirational stories, there is a chapter included on trauma and how it rewires our brain, as well as the effects of Secondary Trauma, especially as it affects someone who is still dealing with their own fallout from traumatic experiences. Find it at bit.ly/firewithinbook

Divergent EDU: Challenging assumptions and limitations to create a culture of innovation

The concept of being innovative can be made to sound so simple. We think of a new idea. But what if the development of the innovative thinking isn't the only roadblock? What if so much of your day is spent solving the issues around you that even the attempt at developing new ideas is not even on your radar? What if you long to have more divergent teachers in your school district or to be that divergent teacher, but you simply don't know where to start? I have developed the foundational levels to the Hierarchy of Needs for Innovation and Divergent Thinking in hopes that the information will help educators find the holes in their foundational levels and fill them. When educators are supported, amazing learning opportunities can happen, and a solid foundation allows for more time to try new ideas, challenge their own assumptions, and teach divergently! Find it at bit.ly/divergent_edu

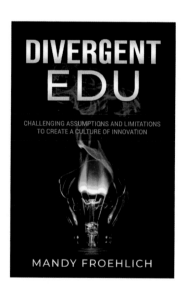

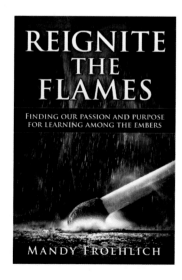

The purpose of this book isn't to judge any educator based on where they are on the continuum of engagement. The purpose is to provide the words that people need to describe their feelings so they can move toward healing. **Reignite the Flames**, the follow-up book to *The Fire Within*, expands on the concepts of:

- Educator engagement and disengagement
- The connection between disengagement and mental health issues like burnout, secondary traumatic stress, and demoralization
- The impact of stress and trauma on our brains and bodies
- And strategies for self-care and re-engagement

There is no denying the challenge of being an educator, but there are opportunities to re-engage and be happy. *Reignite the Flames* provides the vocabulary and the roadmap to help. Find it at bit.ly/reignitetheflames

Made in the USA
Monee, IL
21 June 2021